Who Is Christ for Us?

FACETS

Who Is Christ for Us?
Dietrich Bonhoeffer

The Spirituality of the Psalms
Walter Brueggemann

Biblical Theology: A Proposal
Brevard S. Childs

Christian Faith and Religious Diversity
Mobilization for the Human Family
Edited by John B. Cobb Jr.

The Measure of a Man
Martin Luther King Jr.

The Sayings of Jesus
The Sayings Gospel Q in English
Foreword by James M. Robinson

Visionary Women: Three Medieval Mystics
Rosemary Radford Ruether

The Contemporary Quest for Jesus
N. T. Wright

Who Is Christ
for Us?

Dietrich Bonhoeffer

Translated by Craig L. Nessan
Edited and Introduced by
Craig L. Nessan and Renate Wind

Fortress Press
Minneapolis

WHO IS CHRIST FOR US?

First Fortress Press Edition 2002

Cover and book design: Joseph Bonyata
Cover graphic: copyright © nonstøck inc. Used by permission.
Photo of Dietrich Bonhoeffer, 1930, courtesy Gütersloher Verlagshaus, Germany.

0-8006-3480-2

Manufactured in the U.S.A.   AF 1-3480

06 05 04 03 02 1 2 3 4 5 6 7 8 9 10

Contents

Foreword to the
English Edition

"Who are you, Christ?" Dietrich Bonhoeffer's
question from his 1933 Christology lectures hear-
kens us back to the penetrating question that
Jesus himself posed to his first disciples: "But who
do you say that I am?" (Matt. 16:15). This is the
core Christological question that is placed before
those who seek to learn about Jesus Christ in
every generation. Peter answered the question
confidently, "You are the Messiah, the Son of the
living God." (Matt. 16:16). As he gave his reply,
however, Peter had much to learn yet about the
cost of discipleship that would lead him to the
cross. Did the young Dietrich Bonhoeffer have
any better idea of where his answer to the Christological question would lead him?

The selection of texts by Dietrich Bonhoeffer in
this book leads the reader on a journey with him
to inquire about the identity and way of Jesus
Christ. It is our thesis, as authors of the two
accompanying interpretive essays, that for Bonhoeffer this was not merely an academic question.

1

Although his 1933 Christology lectures were delivered as part of an academic curriculum at the prestigious University of Berlin, they must be interpreted in light of the political events that were unfolding in that same year—the rise of Adolf Hitler and the National Socialist party to power and the immediate attempt to introduce measures to force the church into allegiance to the Third Reich.

Our interpretive essays insist that we view the academic and the political Bonhoeffer as two inseparable dimensions of the same person. The insistence on Christ as the center of history, which runs from the beginning to the end of Bonhoeffer's theological legacy, means that his political commitments are informed by his Christology while his Christology is only realized in political engagement. In this way these early lectures on Christology continue to lay the foundation for both Bonhoeffer's later writings on the cost of discipleship and his decision to participate in the conspiracy to assassinate Adolf Hitler.

Who is Jesus Christ for us? For those of us alive at this moment in history, we must take up this question anew. While we cannot rely on the answers of the generations who have gone before us, our quest can be deeply informed by the example of the martyr Bonhoeffer, whose rigorous efforts at understanding were matched by the courage to risk his convictions in political engagement. It is our conviction that the readers of this book will be similarly challenged both to strenuous thinking about the identity of Jesus

Christ and to courageous activity on behalf of the most vulnerable in contemporary society.

The authors express their gratitude to Michael West of Fortress Press for his editorial direction, Jutta Schwarz for her help with research in Berlin, Kevin Anderson for capable assistance in the preparation of the manuscript, and Tiffany Nichole Broman and Kim Wills for preparation of bibliographic material. We dedicate this book to our students in Nuremberg and Dubuque in the hope that they aspire to a faith active in political engagement.

—*Craig L. Nessan*

Foreword to the German Edition

This ecumenical reader in the Christology of Dietrich Bonhoeffer originated from an ecumenical encounter. At a theological conference of the Central States Synod of the Evangelical Lutheran Church in America on the theology of Dietrich Bonhoeffer, it was noted that frequent references were made by Americans to the Christology lectures of Bonhoeffer that appeared in the United States under the title *Christ the Center*. It was surprising that these lectures belonged to the most frequently read of Bonhoeffer's titles, alongside *Letters and Papers from Prison, The Cost of Discipleship,* and *Life Together*—not only in the circle of experts but even in American congregations.

This was especially surprising because the Christology lectures have found scarcely a detectable echo in the ecclesial life of the Lutheran churches in Germany.

The ecumenical conversation that began with Craig L. Nessan, Professor of Contextual Theology at Wartburg Theological Seminary in Dubuque, is documented in this book. In addition, selected texts from the Christology lectures are presented which, beyond the immediate moment and the needs of an academic lectureship in dogmatics, can be of interest to the contemporary reader. At the same time these texts are accompanied by a number of complementary texts, not from the lectures themselves, that make clear how the Christological statements of Bonhoeffer are intricately connected to his entire theological thinking, his biography, and his times, particularly in the immediate political situation and ecclesial context of the year 1933.

This reader arises out of concern that Bonhoeffer's question—"Who are you, Christ?"—be addressed in the contemporary context of Christian social responsibility and in the newly emerging requirement that the church take a position in such matters.

—*Renate Wind*

Church Struggle and Contemplation: A Rediscovery of Bonhoeffer's Political Christology

Renate Wind

I. "Who are you, Christ?" Bonhoeffer asked this question at the beginning of his Christology lectures in the summer semester of 1933 at the Theological Faculty of the University of Berlin. The question accompanied Bonhoeffer into the last and decisive years of his life. He would pose it anew and even more precisely in a letter to Eberhard Bethge from his prison cell in Tegel on April 30, 1944: "Who is Christ for us today?" In reply Bonhoeffer would offer no simple, generalized answers. Instead he would raise liberating and disquieting questions, opening horizons and empowering a praxis that was inspired by the thought that Christ is "the man for others" and church "is only church when it is there for others." Christology and ecclesiology come together in this twofold assertion, formulated late in Bonhoeffer's life. Together they flow through his thought, alongside his carefully considered praxis or practice of resistance, his ethics, and his dogmatics. His Christology lectures were a step along this path. What role do these lectures play in his life and thought?

II. In Bonhoeffer's dissertation, *Sanctorum Communio,* completed in 1927, the central theme was already sounded. In pursuit of a sustainable community and a practicable way of life for himself, driven also by the necessity both of finding a credible identity as a theologian and scholar, he fused together ecclesiology and Christology in the formula, "Christ existing as community." No matter how impressive this formula at first appears, the distinction between church as professed and practiced, between ideal and reality, could not thereby be adequately expressed. In the end, both the Christological and the ecclesiological affirmations remain abstract. When and how is the community really Christ? How and at what concrete location is Christ existing? It appears that Bonhoeffer gradually sought concrete answers to these initial, interrelated questions in the further stages of his theological reflection. Nevertheless these concretions do not remain mere thought-experiments. Because of these central questions Bonhoeffer's theology is a "theology in performance," a continual reflection on new existential experiences and on political and ecclesial praxis from the viewpoint of faith. Praxis is not an after-the-fact consequence of his theology but the central location for theological understanding.

III. What experiences and praxis inform the Christology lectures of 1933? Already in *Sanctorum Communio,* Bonhoeffer had introduced the question about how the church, which "is" Christ, must develop a new social expression. In rejection of the German Protestant church, which was still bound politically to the fusion of "throne and altar" and sociologically to a certain economic class, he concluded: "The church of the future will not be bourgeois." How then is it to be otherwise constituted? In reliance on dialectical theology, the answer began somewhat radically but was even more abstract: "Totally differently!" In a presentation to the congregation he served as vicar in 1928, Dietrich Bonhoeffer criticized a church that had become a bourgeois edification society, saying that Christ would not have gone to the cross for such a church.

Prompted by the shock of working in an upper-middle class congregation, an initial concretion became clear and increasingly moved into the center of Bonhoeffer's Christology and ecclesiology. The self-understanding and praxis of the community, of the *sanctorum communio,* depends upon Christ the crucified.

IV. Bonhoeffer spent time in 1930 and 1931 at Union Theological Seminary in New York City. He was chilled by the bourgeois white churchliness of conservative America. But in the local communities of the "other America," he found evidence of the church he was searching for. The storefront churches and self-help centers of Harlem and the ecumenical and cosmopolitan atmosphere of the seminary impressed Bonhoeffer. He was moved by the antecedents of the American civil rights movement and by encounter with the representatives of the Social Gospel, who sought to think and practice the commands of Christ in social and political categories. Conversation partners and friends like

Frank Fisher from Harlem, Paul and Marion Lehmann from the "base" communities, and Reinhold Niebuhr, who was denounced by the rightwing fundamentalists as a communist, gave new direction to Bonhoeffer's search for a concrete expression of "Christ existing as community." The friendship with Jean Lasserre, who confronted Bonhoeffer with the commands of the Sermon on the Mount, decisively changed his life. "I believe I know that inwardly I shall be clear and honest with myself only if I truly begin to take seriously the Sermon on the Mount. . . . There just happen to be things that are worth an uncompromising stand. And it seems to me that peace and social justice, or Christ himself, are such things."[1]

V. Bonhoeffer would not identify himself theologically with all the positions of the Social Gospel, the progressive American theological movement begun by Walter Rauschenbush in the early 1900s. Above all, the optimism of its ideology of progress was suspect to him as a Lutheran. Nevertheless there remained decisive impulses: "The impression that has been made on me by today's advocates of the Social Gospel will leave its mark on me for a long time to come."[2]

In Bonhoeffer's subsequent praxis, inspired by the ideas of the Social Gospel, it became concretely noticeable what it meant to be church for others. This concept of the church was not just a mental image. There is such a church, and Bonhoeffer had experienced it in the American local communities. Their praxis would become for him the site of knowledge about the essence of the church and its task.

When in 1933 the Protestant Church in Germany greeted the brutal exclusion of entire social groups as the "restoration of order," Bonhoeffer's was the single voice speaking for the victims. "The church is obligated unconditionally to the victims of every social order, even when they do not belong to the Christian community."[3]

Admiration for the positions and efforts of the American Civil Liberties Union, which litigates on behalf of politically and ethnically excluded citizens, may have been a factor in this thinking. On February 6, 1933, Bonhoeffer wrote to Reinhold Niebuhr that a "horrible cultural barbarity [is threatening], so that we also must immediately form a Civil Liberties Union here." He added, "The way of the church is darker than almost ever before."[4]

VI. The words of the Christology lectures were directed toward the darkness of the church itself. That would, however, only be perceived by those who noticed the overall darkness of German nationalistic swaggering and the pompous machinations of the *Reichskirche,* the officially sanctioned German Christian church. Witnesses report that the lectures drew more than 200 listeners, who hardly missed even one hour, and that the presentation was followed attentively.

> In concentrated dedication to the central
> theme of theology, here was an approach
> that did not pass over the tumultuous events
> of that year indifferently, but rather without
> dealing with them explicitly, communicated
> something for the long haul, something that
> was needed in light of all that would follow. .
> . . What was more urgent than to attain cer-
> tainty regarding this single question: Who
> was Jesus Christ?[5]

At first glance this appears to be a rather traditional academic exercise in systematic theology.
Bonhoeffer never directly uttered a word about
the political situation. Nevertheless for those with
ears to hear, particularly in the sections against
perverted messianic expectation and the theology
of the natural orders of creation that had been
expropriated by the German Christians, Bonhoeffer took a clear stand against the fatal eupho-
ria and the godless pride of the German Protestant
"national revival." Here was a denial of the stance
of the *Reichskirche,* which rejected the revelation
of God in the crucified Christ in favor of "natural"
revelations of God in a people, race, nation,
blood, and soil.

These clear words from Bonhoeffer's Christology lectures sounded again soon in the Bethel
Confession of the church resistance, also formulated in 1933. His words found another echo in
the Theological Declaration of the Confessing
Synod of the Confessing Church held at Barmen
in 1934. At that time Bonhoeffer was isolated,
even within the church opposition, because of his
posture of political resistance. He "went into the

desert for a time" but followed the continuation of the church struggle with burning interest from his foreign pastoral office in London. Earlier he had taken leave of his students with these words: "We must now endure in silence, and set the firebrand of truth to all four corners of the proud German Christian palace, so that one day the whole structure may collapse."[6]

VII. Bonhoeffer's Christology lectures ended with a penetrating assertion that the humiliated and crucified Jesus Christ, both divine and human, is the center of the faith and the community. The church must follow him in humility. The church emerging in that vision is the "church from below" that Bonhoeffer first got to know in America. Now, in the context of Nazi Germany, there emerged a new concrete expression of it among the underprivileged and endangered opposition in the Confessing Church, the movement resisting the German Christians or *Reichskirche*. His experiences in the U.S. sharpened this point, and the impulses from these experiences that took place prior to 1933 should not be overlooked in his mature theology and praxis. The Christology lectures are therefore a result of the experiences he already had, as well as the basis for the emerging communion of saints in the church resistance.

Bonhoeffer, whose lifelong theme was the search for a new social form for the church, immediately after his return from the U.S. was already thinking about what posture the church should take in society. In a memorandum about the Social Gospel he gave a positive evaluation to the independence of the church from the state. "Alongside the separation of church and state there remains a close connection between church and society. . . . The contact of the church with the world of the workers has never been so widely forgotten as in Germany."[7] For the first time there emerges here the much-discussed ecumenical proposal that orthopraxis precedes orthodoxy. Right action precedes right teaching. Not dogma, but life! Connected to this was the awareness that new words for the old gospel must be forged in praxis and that a "nonreligious interpretation" must also be introduced into Christology. Finally, too, the experience here was anchored—in view of social, economic, and political problems and challenges, like the worldwide economic crisis and the impending threat of war—in the notion that confessional and national boundaries must be overcome in favor of an ecumenical praxis that becomes concrete in engagement for peace and justice. For Bonhoeffer this stance was in accordance with discipleship in the sense of the Sermon on the Mount. Therefore it was not first of all grounded on social ethics but rather on Christology.

This clearly separates him from the representatives of the Social Gospel, whom he criticized for not adequately anchoring the principles of their social ethics in Christology. "Christ is the Mediator who reconciles human beings with God and who forgives their sins. The cross and resurrection as acts of God are therefore the center of history."[8] In spite of these reservations, Bonhoeffer's Christ-centered praxis during the years in Berlin before 1933 was influenced decisively by elements of the

Social Gospel. He began an original kind of ecclesial praxis that took him far beyond the boundaries of academic theology. This made him suspect to the theological faculty of Berlin as a
socialist and pacifist. As a pastoral assistant in
Berlin's working district of Prenzlauer Berg, he
made a first attempt with a confirmation class to
become church on the other side of bourgeois
churchliness. Here Christ was preached in the language of Socialist workers' songs. "No one shall
ever deprive you of the faith that God has prepared for you, too, a day and a sun and a dawn
. . . that God wishes us to see the promised land in
which justice and peace and love prevail, because
Christ prevails."[9]

In the same spirit there arose a youth club, pat-
terned after the American settlement movement
with its inspiration in the Social Gospel, a further
attempt to be a faithful community in the middle
of the world. Already in these years there are har-
bingers of what would later appear under other
conditions in the letters from prison. Both were
radically secular contexts. These efforts are hardly conceivable apart from the experienced praxis
of a church from below that had been successful-
ly immunized against all temptations to pervert
the cross of Jesus Christ into a cross of triumph.

VIII. "Who are you, Christ?" Bonhoeffer asked this
question ever anew and always concretely. With
this question he took leave of the successful and
ambitious scholars and their inconsequential theological erudition. He left behind "theological intel-
lectualism," which tries to understand all things
without assuming any responsibility and which

desires to verbalize all things, even the unthink-able, even the cross. He "broke into a dimension in which the unthinkable became a way of life and the other person became 'infinitely important.'"[10]

Because of the hiddenness of God and the incognito presence of the Resurrected One, disci-pleship of Christ became now the only visible sign of his presence. The act of believing became an act of living, as the question about who Christ is came to be connected with the question about where he is concretely to be found here and now. In the moment of greatest existential affliction and haunted by the question whether the safety of American exile was his proper place, Bon-hoeffer wrote in his journal: "Or have I, after all, avoided the place where He is for me?"[11]

The place where Christ would be present for Bonhoeffer was eventually in political conspiracy, in the perilous praxis of a piety that voluntarily assumed guilt, in the encounter with fellow human beings who had been forsaken by the world in the prison at Tegel, and in the hell of the extermina-tion camps. In the perspective of the church from below, Christ became the "man for others" just as the church "is only church when it is there for others." This church explodes the boundaries of a bourgeois institution. It is not an end in itself, not a piece of Western culture. It is no longer con-fined to the language, images, and interpretive categories of the occidental tradition but instead is secular, religionless, and committed to solidar-ity. It exists from the "prayer and action of the righteous" and through a border-crossing ecu-menical movement from below.

IX. This perspective from below, grounded in Christology, was developed in the 1933 Christology lectures and above all further elaborated in the "theology of the letters from prison." It has for a long time been hardly noted in postwar Bonhoeffer scholarship in West Germany. Bonhoeffer's vision of a church that follows Christ into humiliation, that is the church for others, that lives in the world, and that relinquishes state support and the privileges of a state church, was publicly opposed by the restoration efforts on the part of West German Protestantism after 1945. It was otherwise in the German Democratic Republic (East Germany), where the Protestant Church was forced into a new social location within a radically secularized society. "Insofar as the church looks entirely away from itself, it takes seriously the doctrine of justification and the meaning of grace alone and it embodies the service of Jesus to others. . . . The church of Christ is not a church against others, not even *without* others, but also not *as* others."[12]

Bonhoeffer did not become a model for West German Protestantism in this way, even though his theological inheritance found reliable and committed trustees. The ecclesial establishment for a long time had serious difficulty with Bonhoeffer. Hierarchical thought patterns and the state-church mentality were so deeply anchored in the church that martyrdom and resistance activities could not be considered valid. For some, Bonhoeffer was only a fighter in the political resistance, and not a "witness to the faith." For others he was a martyr who could not be a fighter in the resistance.

Ultimately in the official ecclesial version of Bonhoeffer, the political, secular, and subversive Bonhoeffer, the one who was a critic of the church, was intentionally downplayed.

Elsewhere Bonhoeffer encountered a new generation of theologians who began to analyze the inheritance of their fathers critically, even within the church. By the end of the '60s, through several ecumenical developments, the "secular" Bonhoeffer emerged in the theological positions of Harvey Cox and John A. T. Robinson, the political Bonhoeffer figured in the debates over the antiracism program of the World Council of Churches, and the Bonhoeffer of "the view from below" was taken up in the theology of liberation. It is only reasonable that the Bonhoeffer thus portrayed would have hoped for a different public image in the official church.

In the West German Protestantism of the '70s and '80s, Bonhoeffer finally became a "church father" to the ecclesial base communities and a guiding light to the ecumenical drive for peace, justice, and the preservation of the creation. These distinctly different interpretations of Bonhoeffer do not constitute successive stages but rather exist alongside each other even today. Overall this warning still needs to be sounded: not to celebrate Bonhoeffer but to be held accountable to him. Accountability can only be rendered to the entire Bonhoeffer, if one really aims to do justice to his theological inheritance.

As detailed by Craig L. Nessan in this volume, it is striking how differently Bonhoeffer's legacy was received in the U.S. and in West Germany.

Nessan describes how intensively American theology at first dealt with the secular Bonhoeffer, so much so that it was in need of a corrective. This meant making clear Bonhoeffer's theological anchoring in the Lutheran tradition and seeing the Christological foundation of even the secular and nonreligious Bonhoeffer. By contrast, it is still difficult today for German Protestant theologians to look behind Bonhoeffer the Lutheran theologian and *at the same time* to see the secular and political Bonhoeffer. For the first time, through an open ecumenical dialogue, the entire Bonhoeffer comes into view.

X. This ecumenical theological conversation can contribute to a more adequate apprehension of the complexity of Bonhoeffer's thought. Georges Casalis spoke of the legacy of Dietrich Bonhoeffer as an "open invitation" that should stimulate reflection on one's own faith and one's own praxis in church and society.[13] In this connection everything depends on apprehending the deeply theological dimension of Bonhoeffer's politics, so that a clear theological dimension might be brought to the present political response of the church. The prior reception of the Christology lectures makes clear how much this text has been depoliticized by both sides. This is true both of the conservative ecclesial circles, who discovered here only traditional Lutheran dogmatics, and of the politically engaged base-community movement, who could not imagine that lectures in systematic theology could also be charged politically, especially when not a single explicitly political statement was uttered. Would that we could rediscover the political explosiveness of the Christology lectures and see them as a kind of contemplation that intimately accompanied the church struggle and spiritually inspired it! Tiemo Rainer Peters, another partner in this ecumenical conversation, notes the decisive connections among the various levels of interpretation. He makes clear that the Christology lectures, like Bonhoeffer's earlier and subsequent writings, formulate no explicitly political-theological program. They do, however, demonstrate the deeply theological dimension of a secular political praxis: "The question to Christ—'Who are you?'—is posed on behalf of a new humanity, de-ideologized history, and a humane working world. . . . Wherever the community asks this question, they encounter the mystery of the humiliated God and sooner or later must go with him down their own path of humiliation."[14]

It is only logical that a church freed from the strictures of being a state church is more ready to hear this message. This also helps to explain the interest of American Christian congregations in the message of *Christ the Center*. To be sure, there is no commandment according to Bonhoeffer that the church take or not take a certain form. But it does need to orient itself to the humility of the Christ, whether in its social form, its being there for others, its worldliness, or its choosing the perspective from below. The particular historical and political context determines the social location of the church. The criterion of truth is its praxis in the world. "Cut off from its uncompromising engagement, Dietrich Bonhoeffer's pugnacious theology, with an identity that had been forged in a living experiment of what it meant to be church, is not to be accepted. . . . In any case an apolitical and inconsequential interpretation is not faithful to Bonhoeffer."[15]

Interpretation of the whole Bonhoeffer is an ecumenical process in which all are involved. This process will further define what, according to Bonhoeffer, it means to be a Christian: "The prayer and action of the righteous among humanity."

The American Reception: Introduction to Bonhoeffer's *Christ the Center*

Craig L. Nessan

The Dietrich Bonhoeffer who first encountered North American readers was a radical. This was due to the attention most of his early interpreters paid to the challenging and provocative references in his letters and papers from prison. Themes like "the non-religious interpretation of biblical concepts" and "religionless Christianity" in a "world come of age" came to the fore. Publication in 1966 of an English translation of his 1933 Christology lectures, as reconstructed by the able hand of Eberhard Bethge, must be first understood in the context of the times when it appeared.

Only gradually through the 1950s and 1960s did the writings of Bonhoeffer become available in English translation, usually appearing in separate British and American editions. The first book to appear was a small selection of Bonhoeffer's letters from prison, published in the United States under the title *Prisoner for God* in 1953. Other works were translated in steady succession: *Life Together* in 1954, *Ethics* in 1955, *Temptation* also in 1955, *Creation and Fall* in 1959, *The Cost of Discipleship* in 1963 (1959 in London), *Act and Being* in 1961, *The Communion of Saints* in 1963, *No Rusty Swords: Letters, Lectures and Notes, 1928-1936* in 1965, and *The Way to Freedom: Letters, Lectures and Notes, 1935-1939* in 1966. By far the most influential book of Bonhoeffer up to 1966 was, however, the selection of his prison letters, reissued in a revised and enlarged edition in 1967 as *Letters and Papers from Prison.* Since that time, the other most widely known of Bonhoeffer's works in the United States have been *Life Together* and *The Cost of Discipleship.*

During the 1950s, American discussion of Bonhoeffer revolved around his relationship to Rudolf Bultmann's program of "demythologizing," that is, distinguishing the decisive message of the New Testament from its ancient worldview. This took a dramatic turn in the early 1960s, when Bonhoeffer's prison letters became the primary reference point for what became known as "radical theology." William Hamilton, soon to become widely noted as one of the premier "death of God" theologians, published an essay entitled "A Secular Theology for a World Come of Age."[16] In this article, Hamilton referred to Bonhoeffer in establishing the agenda that would occupy a central place in the American theological discussion for the next several years. Bonhoeffer became the prophet of a this-worldly Christianity. Employing lengthy quotes from the prison letters of December 18, 1943, through July 21, 1944, Hamilton argued the contemporary relevance of Bonhoeffer's proposal for the nonreligious interpretation of biblical concepts in a world *etsi Deus non daretur*—as if God were not a given. The contemporary world was deemed the "world come of age," which required a secular theology. Only so could the church fully participate in "the sufferings of God" in the world. Hamilton made explicit reference to the 1933 Christology lectures in this essay, translating and quoting the passage about "the humiliated God-man" who totally assumed human flesh.[17] In this way, the 1933 lectures, four years before their translation as *Christ the Center*, are employed on behalf of the development of what Hamilton calls a "theology of secular culture."[18]

The most influential exposition of these themes was written by John A. T. Robinson, Bishop of Woolwich in England, published in 1963 with the title *Honest to God*.[19] This short and popular book exerted enormous influence not only in England but also in the United States. Robinson aimed to be "honest" to contemporary readers about how it had become necessary in the modern world to talk about God in a new way, in which God would be imaged as radically immanent in the affairs of the world. The time for religious supernaturalism, with its transcendent notion of a God above, was past. Along with Paul Tillich, the main progenitor in this project of reimagining God for a new generation was Dietrich Bonhoeffer. Robinson made repeated reference to "Christianity without religion" and the need for a "nonreligious understanding of God." Bonhoeffer's assertion that "only a suffering God can help us" provided the segue to elaborate an immanental Christology of Jesus as "the man for others," which leaves behind the antiquated Chalcedonian categories:

The life of God, the ultimate Word of Love
in which all things cohere, is bodied forth
completely, unconditionally and without
reserve in the life of a man—the man for
others and the man for God. He is perfect
man and perfect God—not as a mixture of
oil and water, of natural and supernatural—
but as the embodiment through obedience
of "the beyond in our midst," of the transcendence of love.[20]

Following the way of Jesus leads Christians
today along the path of "worldly holiness." Liturgy must not serve as an escape from the world but
as entry into the world. In the ensuing debate over
Robinson's proposals, scarcely a critical word was
uttered about his interpretation of Bonhoeffer.[21]

Other theologians of the period also appealed
to the legacy of Bonhoeffer based almost exclu-
sively on fascinating references from the same
prison letters. Paul M. van Buren wrote in *The
Secular Meaning of the Gospel:* "Bonhoeffer con-
tended that to separate Christian faith and secular
life in the world is to reject the very heart of the
Gospel. . . ."[22] In *The Secular City,* a book that
according to *Newsweek* prophesied "the progressive secularization of the world as the logical out-
come of Biblical religion," Harvey Cox appealed to
the authority of Bonhoeffer's *Letters and Papers
from Prison* both when introducing and summing
up his argument.[23] Most provocatively, Bonhoeffer
became one of the chief authorities for the "death
of God" theologians, Thomas J. J. Altizer and
William Hamilton. Altizer wrote in *Radical Theology and the Death of God:*

> Dietrich Bonhoeffer teaches that the pres-
> ence of Christ can be known only in the
> body of a broken and suffering humanity,
> for the Jesus whom we know is wholly
> detached from the divine attributes of his
> traditional image. For the first time in its
> history, theology is now called to a radical-
> ly kenotic Christology.[24]

In the use made of Bonhoeffer by the radical theologians, there appears no interest in the total
Christological framework out of which Bonhoeffer himself operated in formulating his final theological reflections from prison.

In the same year (1966) that Altizer and Hamilton depicted Bonhoeffer as the grandfather of the
death of God theology, Edwin H. Robertson's
introduction to and John Bowden's translation of
the 1933 Christology lectures under the title
Christ the Center, were published in English. Eberhard Bethge criticized the interpretation of Bonhoeffer by the death of God theologians:

> Wherever this movement referred to Bonho-
> effer, and some theologians like Paul van
> Buren and William Hamilton for a certain
> period relied heavily on him, he was misin-
> terpreted or misunderstood. Some even
> tampered with Bonhoeffer's thought, and
> with an insufficient knowledge of his work,
> did violence to or destroyed his dialectical
> way of expressing himself. What was hap-
> pening was at least made clear by William
> Hamilton once, when in the course of a dis-
> cussion he remarked, "We make a creative
> misuse of Bonhoeffer!"[25]

The appearance of *Christ the Center* marked the beginning of a shift in focus in the interpretation of Bonhoeffer in the United States that was completed with the publication of Eberhard Bethge's comprehensive and now standard biography, *Dietrich Bonhoeffer: Man of Vision, Man of Courage,* in 1970. After the appearance of these works in English, the materials were available for a fuller appreciation of Bonhoeffer's life and thought, overcoming the previously one-sided appropriations of his legacy.

Clearly a central intention behind this English edition of *Christ the Center* was as a corrective to earlier exaggerated interpretations of Bonhoeffer's concern. Edwin H. Robertson explained this in his introduction to the 1966 edition:

> The popular conception of Bonhoeffer is of a theologian who would have done away with all the religious elements of the church and perhaps even with the church itself. As a radical theologian, he is not thought of as one who gets to the root of the matter, as the word would imply, but as an iconoclast. There are certainly many sentences in his *Letters and Papers from Prison* which, when quoted out of context, give credence to this view. Yet he was and remained a Lutheran and a very orthodox churchman.[26]

Publication of *Christ the Center* aimed to be a corrective to the then-current discussion, which paid almost exclusive attention to the provocative statements of the later prison letters. The appearance of this translation placed a demand for more careful attention to the place of Christology

in the entirety of Bonhoeffer's thought, and to
its undergirding what he wrote in the prison
letters. The corrective also forced acknowledgment of the continuity in Bonhoeffer's thinking,
i.e., understanding Bonhoeffer's statements
about the nonreligious interpretation of biblical
concepts in a world come of age not as a radically new vector but as an extension and radi-
calization of his earlier theology. Through the
publication of this volume, it became increasingly clear that the "academic" Bonhoeffer and the
"radical" Bonhoeffer needed to be reconciled in a
more holistic interpretation.

Reviewers of *Christ the Center* in the late '60s
immediately sensed that this book added a necessary new dimension to the popular depiction of
Bonhoeffer. John Godsey, one of the premiere
interpreters of Bonhoeffer in the U.S. over the last
four decades, wrote, "Because it gives background
and substance to much of his later writing, *Christ
the Center* is a book of decisive importance for
interpreting Dietrich Bonhoeffer's thought. . . ."[27]
Other reviewers recognized through these lectures
that Bonhoeffer's Christology was "not far
removed from that of classical Lutheranism"[28]
and that the catch phrases of the late prison letters
"can only be understood or resolved through a
study of Bonhoeffer's christology, in reality his
central subject."[29] Even when Bonhoeffer adopted
the terminology of a "nonreligious interpretation," he never intended this to mean a non-
Christological interpretation.[30] *Christ the Center*
was generally recognized as rooting the whole of

Bonhoeffer's theology deeply in Christology, so that even his stimulating proposals in the prison letters had to be reinterpreted as deeply informed by Christological substance.

One other aspect of the reviews of the 1966 edition deserves mention. Several reviewers documented serious deficiencies in the translation. This resulted in the publication of a new English translation by Edwin H. Robertson in 1978.[31] This was significant not only for the improved rendition but also because of its appearance as a trade paperback in the Harper's Ministers Paperback Library series. This made the lectures far more widely available to the U.S. reading public, especially insofar as this edition was frequently available at popular bookstores.

A major impact of *Christ the Center* on congregational life in the U.S. has been through its influence on the training of two generations of pastors. The availability of these lectures in translation has meant its inclusion among the key texts in seminary courses both on Bonhoeffer and on Christology in general. Through these clergy, the Christological concerns of Bonhoeffer have made an impression, particularly his insistence on the "who" of Jesus Christ as the living person who continues to encounter us today. This Jesus Christ continues to meet us in Word and sacrament. Wherever Jesus Christ appears, he comes as the one *pro nobis*—for us—just as he has always existed as "the man for others." Bonhoeffer's concentration on the humiliation of Christ has undergirded the church's ministry to the excluded and vulnerable in society. Christ is discovered not only at the center of congregational life but also at the center of human existence and at the center of history. It is at this point that one can begin to make legitimate connections with Bonhoeffer's *Letters and Papers from Prison*.

The influence of *Christ the Center* has also been furthered through its inclusion in expositions of Bonhoeffer's theology by authors writing for a popular audience. Two books, one by William Blair Gould and another by Geffrey B. Kelly, each include brief overviews of *Christ the Center* and also include discussion questions for study groups.[32] Selections from *Christ the Center* are also routinely included in anthologies of Bonhoeffer's writings.[33] Such efforts have made the thought of Bonhoeffer widely accessible to U.S. readers as interest in his life and thought continues to increase. This was especially the case in 1995 on the occasion of the fiftieth anniversary of his martyrdom. Beyond the books that deal in a particular way with the 1933 Christology, there exists in English an immense literature on the Bonhoeffer legacy, both popular and scholarly.

The Christology lectures, delivered at Berlin in the summer of 1933, were prepared at a decisive moment in Bonhoeffer's participation in the Confessing Church. This makes his references in *Christ the Center* to the necessity of recovering the concept of heresy as the basis for a confessional church particularly important.[34] Bonhoeffer's resounding appeal to Christ as the basis for his resistance to the Nazis and the German Christians has inspired Christians in recent times also

to recognize the occasion for taking a confessional stance in their own situation. Throughout the
1980s a series of Kairos documents was prepared
to declare the necessity of resistance to developments in and confession of Christ in South Africa,
Central America, and elsewhere.[35] Apartheid, for
example, was named a heresy. This trend led in
1994 to the issuing of *On the Way: From Kairos to
Jubilee* as a Kairos U.S.A. document.[36] Social
oppression, economic injustice, and cultural
breakdown summon Christians to declare "jubilee"
in this moment of crisis and opportunity. To the
extent that U.S. Christians have avoided the confusion between following Christ and American civil
religion, it has been accomplished by a pointed
focus on Christology. Bonhoeffer's stance, fixed as
it was on its Christological center, has exerted significant influence on the development of these
confessing statements.

Although *Christ the Center* has been available
in English translation since 1966 and has been
among those Bonhoeffer texts that have shaped
considerably the course of American theology in
the last thirty years, one can argue that the poten-
tial of these lectures has yet to be realized. What
Bonhoeffer meant by the displacement of God in
a "world come of age" is only beginning to become
manifest in the United States, as modernity and
Constantinian Christianity give way to post-
modernity and post-Christian existence. If the
church is to claim its uniquely Christian identity
and mission during this inexorable shift from
being a privileged majority to being part of the
plurality and one among many minorities in soci-

ety, then Bonhoeffer's Christology will become an even richer resource. Unlike the appropriation of Bonhoeffer by the death of God theologians in naive celebration of the secularization process, the Christian church will need to immerse itself ever more in the arcane discipline of Christian teaching—and there encounter the living person of Jesus Christ. Only by such faithful concentration upon the present, historical, and eternal Christ will the church be prepared for its mission of meeting this same Christ today as the humiliated one, incognito among the poor and suffering ones.

Dietrich Bonhoeffer's Christology Lectures of 1933: Texts in Context

Insofar as the church proclaims Christ, it must fall down in worshipful silence before the unspeakable. God's Word is unspeakable. Speaking of Christ originates in silence. Silence about Christ is the ground of speech. This is what it means to make an obedient response to the revelation of God that occurs in the Word. The speaking of the church through silence is the proper proclamation of Christ. Prayer requires both silence and crying out at the same time, both in the presence of God in response to God's Word.

Dietrich Bonhoeffer, Christology Lectures, 1933
(DBW 12:280)

Jesus Christ, as he is attested for us in Holy Scriptures, is the one Word of God which we have to hear and which we have to trust and obey in life and in death.

We reject the false doctrine, as though the church could and would have to acknowledge as a source of its proclamation, apart from and besides this one Word of God, still other events and powers, figures and truths, as God's revelation.

Thesis 1 of the "Barmen Theological Declaration,"
1934

Who are you? Are you truly God? In Christology it comes down to only these questions. Every possibility of systemization must therefore go astray, for the existence of this Logos means the elimination of my Logos. He *is* the Logos. He *is* the encountering Word. It all depends upon "being"! The question about the who [of Jesus Christ] is the question about transcendence. The question about the how is the question about immanence. Because, however, the one who is being asked about is the very Son himself, the immanent question about the how is never able to comprehend him. To ask how you are possible is a godless question, the question of the serpent. Rather we must ask: Who are you? The question about the who preserves the otherness of the other. The question about the who is at the same time a question about the very existence of the ones posing the question. In the question about the who, the questioners are asking about the boundary of their own being. Should the questioners hear in reply that their Logos has met a boundary, then they have encountered the boundary of their existence. The question about existence is a question about transcendence.

In our daily language the question, "Who are you?" is very common. Nevertheless it is easily changed into the how question. Tell me *how* you are. Tell me *how* you are thinking. Then I can determine *who* you are.

The question about the who is the most basic religious question. It is a question about another person, another being, another authority. It is a question about the love of one's neighbor. The question about transcendence and the question about existence is a question about the neighbor. It is a question about a person. That we are always asking how demonstrates our captivity to our own authority. If we were to ask, "Who are you?" we would be speaking the language of the obedient Adam. Instead we think according to the fallen Adam, asking how.

Are we able to pose the authentic question about the who? And if we do ask about the who, are we able to really mean something other than how? No, we are not able. The mystery of the who remains concealed from us. The ultimate question for critical thought is that it must ask about the who, yet it cannot. This means that one can only legitimately ask about the who after the one who is being asked about has been revealed. That is, one can only ask about the who, provided that the answer has already earlier occurred. And this means furthermore that the Christological question can only be posed in the realm of the church, provided the fact that Christ's claim to be the Word of God is a legitimate claim. Truly there is only one way to seek for God, based upon the knowledge that I already know who God is. There can be no blind search after something like God. I can only seek after something that has already been found. "You would not be searching for me if you had not already found me" (Pascal).

This is clearly the place where our work must begin. In the church, where Christ has revealed himself as the Word of God, the human Logos poses the question: Who are you, Jesus Christ? Logos of God! The answer is already given. The church receives it every day anew. It remains a task of the human Logos only to understand fully the question that has been asked, to probe and analyze it according to its very being. Nevertheless, the abiding question is: "Who?"

Dietrich Bonhoeffer, Christology Lectures, 1933
(DBW 12:282–284)

Once again today I ask myself,
Who you were or are,
What you want.
Many know it better,
Some follow after you.
But how did you come even to me?
For I am not the one
Whom you need.
Nevertheless,
Nevertheless
I cannot get away
From you

Kurt Marti

The question of existence asks about the transcendence of the human being. Transcendence is truly the boundary of the being that has been given to me. The question that asks about my existence and places it in question is at the same time the question of transcendence, because my very own existence is being put in question from the perspective of transcendence. Theologically expressed, human beings only know who they are from the perspective of God. If now the question about the who is the only question, the question that I ask about something beyond my own being, then it becomes the only question that asks about transcendence and existence. The question about the who can never be answered by human beings alone. The question cannot be answered from within existence itself, because human beings cannot themselves escape from the confines of their existence. They remain entirely bound to it, seeing only their own image in the mirror.

Human beings annihilate the who that stands as their counterpart. Who are you? Thus they question Jesus. He remains silent. Human beings cannot wait for the answer. They kill him. The human Logos cannot endure the counter-Logos, knowing that one of them must die. Therefore the human Logos murders the One who is encountered, the Logos of Jesus Christ who has posed the radical question, and chooses to live instead without answering the question about existence and about transcendence. Yet human beings can no longer murder the counter-Logos; he has been raised from the dead. Either they cannot perceive him at all, or they perceive him as the one who asks them, "Who are you?" Because Christ is the Son, the question posed to Christ, about who you are, has already been answered.

Even today human beings cannot avoid meeting the figure of Jesus Christ. They must come to grips with him. Life and death, salvation and damnation, hang in the balance of this encounter. Looked at from the outside, this does not appear to be the case. From the perspective of the church, this is the assertion upon which everything else rests: "There is salvation in no one else." There have been thousands of attempts to resist this encounter and thereby evade it. Christ in the world of the working class has apparently been eliminated, as have been the church and middle-class society in general. There appears to be no occasion to provide for an appropriate locale for the encounter with Jesus. The church is an institution for promoting stupidity and the sanctioning of the capitalist system. And yet this is not the case. Jesus must be distinguished from his church and its religion. The working class means more by saying, "Jesus is a good man," than when the middle class says, "Jesus is God." Jesus the worker is present in the shops of the factories. In politics, he is the perfect idealist. In the life of the working class, he is the good guy. He is in the midst of the working class, a fighter in the ranks of the working class struggling against the enemy, capitalism.

Thus Jesus Christ enters into our time, meeting all classes and occupations, being queried ever anew: Who are you? Then, too, those who feel themselves threatened by this question kill him ever anew. All of this is an attempt to be finished somehow with Christ. The theologian also tries to do this. Everywhere the Son of Man is betrayed by the kiss of Judas. To be finished with Christ means to kill him, to crucify him, to dishonor him, to bend down with the persecutors and say: "Greetings, Rabbi!"

There are only two possibilities in the encounter between human beings and Jesus: either the human being must die or the human being must kill Jesus. Therefore the question, "Who are you?" still remains ambiguous. It can be the question of the one who is convicted by the question as it has been posed and instead of hearing an answer,

hears rather the counter-question: "Who then are
you?" Only in this case is it the question of someone oriented toward Jesus. The question about the
who can only properly be posed to Jesus, when
someone is oriented toward him. In this case,
however, it is not the human being who is finished with Jesus but Jesus who is finished with
the human being. Strictly understood, the question about the who is therefore only uttered in
faith, where it receives its answer. Insofar as the
Christological question remains a question of our
Logos, it remains forever bound by the ambiguity
of the how question. However, insofar as it exists
as an act of faith, it has the possibility of becoming the who question.

Dietrich Bonhoeffer, Christology Lectures, 1933
(DBW 12:286–288)

In gloomy times of bloody confusion
Ordered disorder
Planful willfulness
Dehumanized humanity
When there is no end to the unrest in our
cities:
Into such a world, a world like a slaughter-
house—
Summoned by rumors of threatening deeds
of violence

To prevent the brute strength of the short-
sighted people
From shattering its own tools and
Trampling its own bread-basket to pieces—
We wish to reintroduce
God.

A figure of little glory,
Almost of ill repute,
No longer admitted
To the sphere of actual life:
But, for the humblest, the one salvation!
Therefore we have decided
To beat the drum for Him
That He may gain a foothold in the regions
of misery
And His voice may ring out clearly among
the slaughterhouses.
And this undertaking of ours is surely
The last of its kind. A last attempt
To set Him upright again in a crumbling
world, and that
By means of the lowest

Bertolt Brecht
"Saint Joan of the Stockyards," 1931

Everything depends on whether one thinks that
Jesus Christ is the idealistic founder of a religion
or the very Son of God. Nothing less than the life
and death of the human being hangs in the balance. If he was the idealistic founder of a religion,
then I can be inspired by his accomplishments
and motivated to imitate his zeal, but my sin is
not forgiven. In this instance God is still angry
with me, and I am under the power of death.
Jesus' work leads me in this case to total despair
about myself.

If, however, the work of Christ is the work of
God, then I am not summoned to act like God or
to imitate God zealously, but instead I am convicted by this work as one who in no way can do

it by myself. Rather I have found all at once the gracious God through this Jesus Christ, in this knowledge and in this work. My sin has been forgiven. I am not dead but alive. It depends therefore on the person of Christ, whether his work is understood as passing away according to the old world of death or whether it is eternal according to a new world of life.

But how shall the person of Christ be recognized apart from his work? This objection indicates the deepest error. Even the work of Christ is not unambiguous. It remains susceptible to the most different explanations. His work admits also this interpretation: that he is a hero and the cross is the perfect act of conviction by a courageous man. There is no moment in his work to which one can clearly refer and say that here Jesus on the basis of his work is clearly and undoubtedly recognizable as the Son of God. This is the situation that the Son has assumed by taking on flesh, that he wants to do his work incognito in the midst of the ambiguity of history. The twofold impossibility of recognizing the person of Jesus through his work is grounded in this incognito: first, because the deduction of his person from his work is humanly impossible in general and, secondly, because Jesus is God and a direct deduction of God from history is never possible.

If this way of recognition is closed, then there is only one other attempt by which to find an approach to Jesus. And this approach can only occur at that place where the person reveals himself to me according to his own being. His person and also his work are only disclosed to me through the revelation of Christ.

Thereby the theological priority of the Christo-logical question is shown to be prior to the soteri-ological question. I must first know who someone *is* that does something before I know what that someone has done. Nevertheless it would be wrong to draw the conclusion of separating the person and work. We are asking here only about the question of the epistemological connection of work and person, not about the question of the real connection of person and work. This separa-tion is only necessary in terms of theological method. For the theological question according to its essence can only be asked about the whole Christ. It is the historically whole Christ who is addressed and who replies. For the sake of Chris-tology he is not asked about his acts but about his being. Expressed abstractly, the personal being-structure of the whole historical Christ is the object of Christology.

Dietrich Bonhoeffer, Christology Lectures, 1933
(DBW 12:290f.)

What inexorably moves me is the question: what Christianity is or especially who Christ really is for us today. The time when one could express this to others through words—be they theological or pious words—is gone. Likewise gone is the time of inwardness and of the conscience; that means in general the time of religion. We are entering into a fully religionless time. People, such as they once were, can simply no longer be religious.... How can Christ also become the Lord of the reli-gionless? . . . What do the church, congregation, preaching, liturgy, or the Christian life mean in a religionless world? . . . How do we speak "secularly" about "God"? How can we be "religionless-secularized" Christians? How can we be *ek-klesia,* those who are called out, without understanding ourselves religiously as the privileged ones, but rather as those who belong entirely to the world? Christ then becomes no longer the object of religion but something entirely different, truly the Lord of the world.

Dietrich Bonhoeffer, Letter from Tegel Prison, 1944
(DBW 8:402–405)

Jesus as the crucified and risen one is at the same time the present Christ. This is the first affirmation: Christ is the present historical Christ. His presence is to be understood temporally and spatially. Both come together in the concept of the church, now and here. Christ in his personhood is present in the church, present only as person. The presence of Christ therefore abides in the church. Only because Christ is the present Christ are we still able to interrogate him. Only because proclamation and sacraments take place in the church are we able to ask about Christ.

The presence of Jesus Christ requires these assertions: Jesus is entirely human, as well as another, Jesus is entirely God, otherwise he would not be present. Thereby from the presence of Christ we draw a twofold conclusion, that he is both human and God. The question about how the human Jesus could at the same time be with us is therefore impossible. As if this Jesus could exist in isolation! Just as impossible is the question about how God could exist in time. As if there could be such an isolated God! The only sensible question is: Who is present, contemporaneous, at hand? The answer is Jesus, human and God. I do not know anything about who the human Christ is if at the same time I do not consider the God-Christ, and vice-versa. God in timeless eternity is not God. Jesus Christ in time-bound humanity is *not* Jesus Christ. Rather God is God in the humanity of Jesus Christ. Only in Jesus Christ is God present.

The starting point for Christology must be the God-human. The space-time continuum is not only the human but also the divine determination of Christ. The God-human, who is present in space and time, is hidden in the "form of the flesh" (Rom. 8:3). The presence of Christ is a hidden presence. But it is not that God is hidden in the human, rather the God-human as a whole is hidden, and the principle of hiddenness is precisely the "form of the flesh."

Thereby the problem is altered: not the relationship of the divine and human in Jesus Christ, but the relationship of the already given God-human to the "form of the flesh." The God-human is present in the form of the flesh, in the form of a stumbling block. The hiddenness of the *present* Christ takes place for us in the proclamation of the church. Jesus Christ, as the already existing God-human, is present in the church only in the offensive form of its proclamation. The proclaimed Christ is the real Christ. The offensiveness does not occur in the hiddenness of God, but in the hiddenness of the God-human. The humanity of Christ and the humiliation of Christ are to be dis-

tinguished from one another entirely and carefully. The human Jesus Christ is both the humiliated
one and the risen one. Only Jesus Christ as the
humiliated one is offensive. The doctrine of the
stumbling block does not have its place in the
doctrine of the incarnation of God but rather in
the doctrine of the state of humiliation of the
God-human. This means for us that the presence
of the God-human as the resurrected one, i.e., the
risen one, is at the same time the presence of the
humiliated Christ.

Present in the threefold form of word, sacrament, and congregation, the fundamental question about the presence of Christ has not been
answered. The question cannot be: How can the
human Jesus or the God Jesus be here at the same
time? The question must go like this: On the basis
of what structure of personhood is Christ present
in the church? If one responds that it is on the
basis of God-humanity, that is right, but not yet
explicit enough. It is contained in the *pro me*
structure. The being of the person of Christ is
essentially a relatedness to me. The being of Christ
is a being *pro me*. This *pro me* should not be
understood as an effect that proceeds from him,
but it should be understood as the being of the
very person. This means that I can never think of
Jesus Christ as being-unto-himself but rather only
in his relatedness to me. Again this means that I
can only think about Christ in the existential
relation to him and moreover within the congregation. It is not about Christ in himself or even in the
congregation, but the Christ who is the real Christ
is the one present in the congregation *pro me*.

The God-human Jesus Christ is the one who is present to the church in his person through his *pro me* structure as word, sacrament, and congregation.

Dietrich Bonhoeffer, Christology Lectures, 1933
(DBW 12:291f., 294–297)

The Christian church is the congregation of the brethren, in which Jesus Christ acts presently as the Lord in Word and sacrament through the Holy Spirit. As the church of pardoned sinners, it has to testify in the midst of a sinful world, with its faith as with its obedience, with its message as with its order, that it is solely his property, and that it lives and wants to live solely from his comfort and from his direction in the expectation of his appearance.

We reject the false doctrine, as though the church were permitted to abandon the form of its message and order to its own pleasure or to changes in prevailing ideological and political convictions.

Thesis 3 of the "Barmen Theological Declaration,"
1934

What it means that Christ is the Word is that he is the truth. Truth is only in the Word and through the Word. The Spirit is originally Word, not power, deed, or feeling. "In the beginning was the Word and through the Word are all things done." The Spirit is power and deed only as Word.

It is the truth, as the Word of God, that destroys and creates. Naturally God has the freedom to do things that we do not understand. God has the freedom to be revealed in other ways. But God has chosen to be revealed in the Word. And God is not able to speak to human beings other than through this Word. God has chosen to be bound. God is not willing that this Word be changed.

That Christ is the Word and not a stone means that Christ is there for the sake of human beings. God encounters the human in the Logos because the human being has a Logos. The truth of the human Logos is thereby originally in the Word, because the Word alone mediates clear and unambiguous meaning. Something is accepted as being generally valid based on its clarity and ability to attain a consensus. What entering into this human Logos means is the humiliation of Jesus Christ.

Christ as the Word of God is distinct and different from the human Logos, insofar as Christ is the Word in the form of the living Word for human beings, while the human word takes the form of an idea. These are the two forms of the Word generally: address and idea. But each excludes the other. Our human thinking knows only the one form of the Word as an idea. It belongs to the notion of an idea that it is universally accessible. The idea is simply there. The human being can accept it and acquire it piece by piece.

The Word exists in dramatic contrast to this, not as an idea but as address. If the word as an idea remains essentially isolated by itself, as address it is only possible as a Word between two, as both address and response, in responsibility. It is not atemporal but occurs within history. Therefore it is not general and accessible to all at every moment, but it occurs wherever there exists the address of one to another. The Word remains subject entirely to the freedom of the one who speaks. It is in its essence unique and ever new. It belongs to its character as address that it desires community. It belongs to its character as truth that it seeks community only where it can establish the other in the truth. Truth in this case is something that happens between two and does not abide eternally in itself. Truth happens only in the community of two. Christ as the Word of God in the sense of address does not mean Christ as an atemporal truth but truth that breaks in upon us in the concrete moment as the address of God to us. Christ is thus not atemporal and generally accessible like an idea, but Christ will only be perceived as Word where he lets himself be perceived. That means it all depends on Christ's freedom to reveal or to hide himself from me. Only the Father in heaven reveals Christ, when and where God wills. Christ as Word brings to expression the contingency of his revelation and at the same time the connection with human beings through his Word. Christ as God's address is essentially *pro me*.

In Christ we are not dealing with a new concept of God or a new moral teaching. We are dealing with God's personal address, through which God summons human beings to responsibility.

"I am the way and the truth and the life." This occurs as the absolutely unique possibility of the revelation of God in the One who is the Word in his person.

This Christ who is the Word in person is present in the Word of the church or as Word of the church. His presence is, according to its essence, his existence as preaching. If that were not so, then the exclusive place would not be ascribed to preaching that has been given to it by the Reformation. Preaching is the poverty and the riches of our church. Preaching is the form of the present Christ to which we are bound and on which we must hold. If the whole Christ is not in the preaching, then the church is shattered. The human word and God's Word do not relate in mutual exclusion, but the Word of God, Jesus Christ as the incarnate Word of God, is God's Word that has entered into the humiliation of the human word. Thus Luther says: "You should point to and speak about this human being, for this one is God." We say that you should point to and speak about this human word, for this is God! Christ is in the church as spoken word in the twofold form of preaching and sacrament.

Dietrich Bonhoeffer, Christology Lectures, 1933
(DBW 12:297–300)

We live
Word by word
Tell me
You dearest

Friend
Of mine named
Thou.

Rose Auslaender

> We can only speak with God,
> if we wrap our arms around the world.
>
> Martin Buber

Christ is entirely Word; sacrament is entirely Word. Sacrament is to be distinguished from the Word, insofar as sacrament has its own realm of existence in the church.

Sacrament is the Word of God, for it is proclamation of the Gospel, and exactly through the Word a holy and signifying act. The promise of the "forgiveness of sins" makes the sacrament what it is. Whoever believes the Word in the sacrament has the entire sacrament.

The Word in the sacrament is an enfleshed Word. The sacrament is the form of the Word, becoming sacrament when God speaks through it. The bodily form of the sacrament occurs only through the Word, occurs only as Word, as enfleshed Word. The sacrament in the form of nature should grasp human beings in their nature.

The fallen creation is no longer the creation at the first Word. The "I" is no longer the "I" as God intended it. Similarly, *tribe* is no longer *tribe, history* is no longer *history, church* is no longer *church*. Thereby the continuity of Word and creature has been lost. Therefore the natural world is no longer a transparent world. Therefore the entire creation is no longer sacrament. Sacrament occurs only there where God in the midst of the creaturely world names, claims, and sanctifies an element through God's own special Word, in that God gives it that name. Thus through the claim of God this element becomes what it is. Thus it happens in the Lord's Supper that God sanctifies the elements of bread and wine through God's Word. God's Word, however, means Jesus Christ. Through Jesus Christ the sacrament is sanctified and understood. God has become bound to the sacrament through God's Word. That means that Jesus Christ is someone who is bound to the sacrament. The whole God-human Jesus Christ is present in the sacrament.

The sacrament as Jesus Christ is essentially Word. Contrary to the attempt to understand Christ as a doctrine or as a generalized truth, the church affirms Christ as sacrament, and this means that he is not doctrine according to his essence. Thereby an error is avoided, as though Christ were an idea and not at the same time history and nature.

However, not every natural object and every bodily thing is determined to become sacrament. The presence of Christ remains limited to preaching and sacrament. Why exactly are these sacraments? The Protestant church says it is because they are acts instituted by Jesus Christ. Institution through Jesus Christ does not mean anything else except the risen and present Christ has given them to his congregation. They are not symbols but rather the Word of God. They do not *signify* anything, but rather they *are* something.

The sacrament is not the veiling of a bodily Word of God in the body, so that the sacrament becomes a second incarnation. Instead the Word of God become flesh, the incarnate God, the God-human is now in the sacrament in the form of a stumbling block. God is revealed in the flesh but also concealed in a stumbling block. This means that the question about the presence of Christ in the sacrament may not be analyzed as the question about the humanity and divinity of Christ but rather as the question about the presence of the God-human in the form of the humiliation, of the stumbling block.

Who is the Christ who is present in the sacrament? The God-human, the Risen One! Jesus exists such that he is existentially the one who is present in the sacrament. His way of being in the sacrament is not a matter of a special willing on his part, nor a property; rather he exists essentially as sacrament in the church, exactly because he is the humiliated one. His way of being in the sacrament is his present humiliation; his existence is a humiliated existence.

What is the difference between the Christ who is present *in* us *as* sacrament and the Christ who is present *in* us *as* Word? Nothing. It is the same forgiving and judging Christ who is Word and who abides in both locations. Christ is present to us in the sacrament in the sphere of the tangible nature of our body. He is here next to us as creature, in our midst as our brother. He is, as sacrament, the restored creation of our spiritual-bodily existence; he is the new creature, exactly as he is the human one who is humiliated in the bread and the wine. Because he, as the new creature, is in bread and wine, therefore bread and wine are the new creation. Bread and wine are essentially and really the new nourishment of those who receive in faith. They are, as restored creation, no longer in themselves or for themselves but for other human beings. This being-for-other-human-beings is their newly created way of being. Christ is present in the sacrament as Creator of nature and as creature at the same time. As Creator, he is present as *our* Creator, who makes our very selves into new creatures through this new creature. The question about *how* this can be is to be transformed into the question about who is the one who is doing this. And the answer resounds: the historical, crucified, resurrected, and ascended Jesus of Nazareth, the God-human, but here revealed as brother and Lord, creature and creation.

Dietrich Bonhoeffer, Christology Lectures, 1933
(DBW 12:300–302, 304f.)

The church teaches that in the beginning God created the world out of nothing and is its Lord. We receive this faith from the proclamation of the revelation of the Triune God alone, as the church on the basis of the Holy Scriptures testifies to us. According to what occurs through this testimony, pious and natural knowledge is unable to grasp neither God as creator nor the world as creation....

Faith and natural knowledge are therefore no longer one, because we live in a fallen world. . . .

Therefore we are dependent for knowledge of God upon God's self-revelation alone, testified through the Holy Scriptures and proclaimed through the preaching of the church. . . .

We reject the false teaching that this world, as it is, corresponds to the original will of God for creation and therefore must be affirmed as unbroken. . . .

We reject the false teaching that struggle is the fundamental law of the original creation and that therefore a competitive attitude is a law of God established from the original creation. . . .

We reject the false teaching that God speaks to us in an unmediated way at a certain "historical hour" and is revealed in an unmediated act in creation. . . .

We reject as an enthusiast's interpretation of history the false teaching that the voice of the tribe is the voice of God.

From the "Bethel Confession," 1933
(DBW 12:371–374)

Christ as Word and sacrament is present as congregation. The presence of Christ as Word and sacrament relates to Christ as congregation, as do reality and form. Christ is the congregation by virtue of his being *pro me*. He acts as the new humanity. Between ascension and *parousia* the congregation is his form. What does it mean that Word and sacrament are congregation?

Word, as Word of God, is congregation. That means it has temporal and spatial existence. It is not only the weak word of human teaching but instead the powerful Word of the Creator. It creates for itself the form of the congregation, insofar as it speaks. Congregation is Word of God insofar as the Word of God is God's revelation. Only because the congregation itself is the Word of God, can it understand the Word of God alone. One only understands revelation on the basis of revelation. The Word is in the congregation insofar as the congregation is a receiver of the Word.

The sacrament is also both in the congregation and there as congregation. Beyond the Word it has in itself already a bodily form. This form of his embodiment is the body of Christ himself and is as such at the same time the form of the congregation. This is no mere image. The congregation *is* the body of Christ. It really is what it says it is. The concept of the body applied to the congregation is not a functional concept that relates itself to the members, but instead it is a concept about the way of existence of the present, risen and humiliated Christ.

Insofar as the congregation is congregation, it no longer sins. But it remains in the world of the old Adam. As such it is still under the eon of sin. Christ's being as congregation is, like his being as the Word, a being in the form of the stumbling block.

> Dietrich Bonhoeffer, Christology Lectures, 1933
> (DBW 12:305f.)

The various offices in the church do not establish a dominion of some over the others; on the contrary, they are for the exercise of the ministry entrusted to and enjoined upon the whole congregation.

We reject the false doctrine, as though the church, apart from this ministry, could and were permitted to give to itself, or allow to be given to it, special leaders vested with ruling powers.

> Thesis 4 of the "Barmen Theological Declaration,"
> 1934

If we inquire about the location of Christ, we are inquiring about the structure of the "where" in relationship to the structure of the "who" of Christ. Where is he standing? For me, in my place, where I should be standing. He is standing there because I am unable to stand there. That means he is standing at the boundary of my existence and at the same time in my place. That is a way of expressing the fact that I am separated by an impassable boundary from the I that I should be. The boundary lies between my old and my new I, exactly in the middle between me and me. Christ, as the boundary, is at the same time for me a rediscovered center. The boundary as boundary can only be viewed from the far side of the boundary. It all depends upon human beings, insofar as they recognize their own boundary in Christ, seeing in this boundary at the same time their new center. That is the essence of Christ's person, to be in the center. The one who exists in the center is the same one who is present in the church as Word and sacrament. If we bring the question about the where back toward the question about the who, we attain the answer: Christ, as the one who exists *pro me,* is the Mediator. That is his essence and his way of existence.

Being-in-the center means three things: being there for human beings, being there for history, and being there for nature. It is Christ's *pro me* translated into the structure of the *where.* His ability to mediate must be demonstrated in that he can be understood as the center of existence, history, and nature.

The center of our existence is not the center of our personality. Christ is not the tangible center but the believed center. The center in a fallen world is, however, at the same time boundary. Human beings stand between law and fulfillment. They have the law but not the possibility of the fulfillment of the law. Christ as the center means that he is the fulfilled law. Thereby he is at the same time the boundary and the tribunal over human beings. Yet Christ is not only the end of existence, i.e., boundary, but the beginning of the new existence, and that means center. To say Christ is the center of our existence means that he is the tribunal and the justification.

Dietrich Bonhoeffer, Christology Lectures, 1933
(DBW 12:306f.)

Great programs always only lead us back to where we ourselves already are. However, we should allow ourselves only to be found where Christ is. We truly can be nowhere else than where he is. Whether you work over there or I work in America, both of us are only where Christ is. He takes us along. Or, have I perhaps avoided the place where he is? The place where he is for me?

Dietrich Bonhoeffer, "Journal of the Trip to America,"
1939 (DBW 15:218)

Christ is the center of history, in that he is its boundary and center at the same time. That means history is lived between promise and fulfillment. History bears a promise within it, to become the people of God, as well as the promise of the Messiah. This promise has come alive

everywhere. History is lived only toward the fulfillment of this promise. This means history is
essentially messianic history. The meaning of history is nothing else than the coming of the Messiah. However, it remains under the promise like the
individual under the law, i.e., it can by itself not
fulfill the promise. History seeks to be glorified in
the Messiah. History agonizes in the direction of
the impossible fulfillment of a distorted promise.
History knows about its messianic destiny, but it
is frustrated by it. Only in one place does the
thought gain a foothold against the stream of the
messianic promise, that the Messiah could not be
the visible and tangible center of historical existence, but that the Messiah must be and will be
the center of history that has been established, yet
hidden by God. Thus Israel with its prophetic hope
stands alone among the peoples. Thus Israel
becomes the location where God fulfills this
promise. One cannot prove that Christ is the Messiah; instead he can only be proclaimed. This
statement means that Christ is at the same time
both the destruction and the fulfillment of the
messianic expectation of history. It is destroyed
because its fulfillment occurs in a hidden way. It
is fulfilled insofar as the Messiah is now really
there. The meaning of history is intertwined with
an event that occurred hidden in the depths of
human life on the cross. The meaning of history
occurs in the humiliated Christ. With this every
other claim about history is finished, judged and
destroyed. History with all its promises is here
brought to its boundary. According to its essence
it is at its end. However, thereby the boundary is

at the same time again the center. Thus also Christ is here the boundary and center of the being of history. Exactly there where history should stand, Christ stands before God. So Christ is also the mediator of history.

The church should be understood as the center of history. The church is the center of a history that is made by the state. The church as the center must be understood as the hidden center of the state. The church as the present Christ preserves its being in the center not insofar as it is placed in the visible center of the state, not insofar as it becomes a state church. It preserves its position within the state not by its visible position within the governmental sphere, but only insofar as the church judges and justifies the state, for it is the essence of the state to bring the meaning of a people toward fulfillment through action that creates law and order. Thus in every state the messianic concept underlies the concept of creating order.

The church as the center of the state is now the boundary of the state insofar as it must recognize and proclaim the overcoming of every human promise through Christ's cross. It proclaims by the cross both the affirmation of order as well as also its ultimate overcoming and annulment through God's entrance and need to die in history.

Dietrich Bonhoeffer, Christology Lectures, 1933
(DBW 12:308f.)

Interviewer: The prophecy of the arrival of the Messiah remains for the Jews still unfulfilled. How would the world be transformed if this prophecy came true?

Shalom Ben-Chorin: The world would become the kingdom of God, the kingdom of peace, right-eousness, and love among all people. The nations would mold their swords into plowshares and their spears into pruning hooks, as it was foretold by Isaiah and Micah. No nation would ever again lift a sword against another, and no one would again study the art of war.... I see that as the goal of history, and if I could not believe in it, then I would have no hope.... I think this waiting for the kingdom of God is only meaningful when it is not a passive but rather an active waiting. When we know that we are summoned to realize works of peace, righteousness, and love in our lives. Rabbi Tarphon expressed it very beautifully in the say-ing of the Fathers: "It is not yours to complete the work, but you are not freed from beginning it."

From an interview with Shalom Ben-Chorin

It is not the church but the state that creates and changes the law. Too much law and order is jux-taposed against too little law and order. This means that the state has so extended its authority that it steals from the Christian proclamation and Christian faith its own right. The church must resist this presumption by the governmental order exactly because of its better understanding of the state and the limits of state actions. The state that endangers Christian proclamation denies itself. This indicates a threefold possibility for ecclesial action over against the state. First, there is the questioning of the state about whether the char-acter of its action is legitimate, that is, to call the state to responsibility. Second, there is service to the victims of state action. The church is obligated unconditionally to the victims in every civil order, even when they do not belong to the Christian congregation.... The third possibility consists of this, not only to tend to the victims under the wheel, but to stick a rod in the spokes of the wheel itself. Such action would be inherently political action by the church and is only then possible and requisite when the church sees that the state has failed in its function of creating law and order.

Dietrich Bonhoeffer, The Church and the Jewish
Question, 1933 (DBW 12:353f.)

Christ is the new creature. Christ as the new creature demonstrates that all other creatures are old creatures. Nature stands under the curse that God placed upon Adam's field, for it was the original duty of nature to be and to proclaim the Word of God. Now, as a fallen creature, it is a silent, enslaved, bound, and subject creature, a creature in guilt and under the loss of freedom; a creature that looks forward to a new freedom. Thus nature is between slavery and liberation, slavery and redemption. Nature will therefore not be reconciled but redeemed for freedom. What else are the catastrophes of nature than the stifled will of nature seeking to make itself free, to become by its own power a new creature?

In the sacraments of the church the old creature is liberated from its slavery for a new freedom. Christ, as the redeeming creature, cannot be proven through nature but can only be preached. The enslaved creature is, however, only redeemed in hope. A sign has been established for the

enslaved creature, in that elements of the old creature have become elements of the new creature.
How so? As they are liberated from their silence
and from their interpretation by human beings.
These elements say for themselves what they are.
Only in the sacrament is Christ the center of nature
as the mediator between nature and God.

For Christ, as the center of human existence,
history, and nature, these three are never abstract
or to be separated from each other. Human existence is in fact history and nature at the same
time. Christ as the center means Christ, as the
mediator of the enslaved creation, is the fulfillment of the law and the liberation from this slavery for all humanity. He can only be all that
because he is the one who is *pro me,* taking my
place for me before God. Christ as the mediator is
exactly the end of the old and fallen, and the
beginning of the new world of God.

Dietrich Bonhoeffer, Christology Lectures, 1933
(DBW 12:310f.)

The church teaches that God in divine patience
preserves and allows human beings to live in the
fallen world. To protect human beings from the
intemperance of their self-seeking and their own
self-destruction, God forces human life into stable
orders. These orders are not the orders of the original creation but orders in which God preserves
the life of human beings for the sake of the future
of Christ and the new creation. . . .

We reject the false teaching that we ourselves
are capable of restoring to its purity the order of

creation that has been destroyed by sin. The world is restored only in Christ.

From the "Bethel Confession," 1933 (DBW 12:375, 379)

The present Christ is the historical Christ. This very one is the historical Jesus. If that were not so, then we would say with Paul that our faith is in vain, then our church would lose its substance. How do I become certain about the historical fact of Jesus Christ in an absolute way? Obviously the historical method is here overtaxed. There is no historical passage to the person of Jesus that would be obligatory of faith. Passage to the historical Jesus goes only through the resurrected one, through the Word of the self-authenticating risen Christ.

From this viewpoint the word of history that seeks to defend or deny Christ is irrelevant. History is known in faith from the viewpoint of eternity, not from within itself.

Then too it must be maintained that the testimony to Jesus as the risen one is nothing different from what is handed down through the Bible. Even as believing human beings we remain sober and practical. We must read this book of books with every human method. However, throughout the fragile Bible, God encounters us as the risen one. As long as we are on earth, we must deal with the limitations of historical criticism. The historicity of Jesus exists for us under the two aspects of both history and faith.

Dietrich Bonhoeffer, Christology Lectures, 1933 (DBW 12:311, 313–315)

I bury myself in work in a very unchristian and immodest way. A crazed ambition, which some have noticed about me, makes life difficult. . . . Then something else happened, something that up to this day has changed and rearranged my life. I came for the first time to the Bible . . . I had already often preached; I had already seen much of the church, even spoken and written about it— and still I had never become a Christian, but instead was very furiously and unrestrainedly my own Lord. . . . Also I had never prayed, or only very little. I was with utter abandonment entirely content with myself. The Bible has liberated me from that, and especially the Sermon on the Mount. Since that time everything has become different.

Dietrich Bonhoeffer, Letter to Elisabeth Zinn, 1936
(DBW 14:112f.)

Luther speaks about the divinity and humanity of Jesus, as if they were one nature. For him it is about understanding the humanity of Christ as divinity. The teaching about the *genus majestaticum* derives from this. This teaches that the human nature was permeated with the divine and maintains the attributes of the divine nature. For Luther, Jesus and Christ are not kept separate from each other. Because one senses the danger that one here is talking about a deified human being, one then adds the teaching about the two states of Christ to this teaching about the *genus majestaticum*. This Jesus Christ has passed through two different states, the state of humiliation and the state of exaltation. The doctrine of the two states is useful in order to speak together about the historical Jesus and the redeemer Jesus Christ. The subject of the humiliation is the incarnate one, according to Lutheran Orthodoxy, not the incarnating one. The incarnate one enters freely into humiliation. Christ's nature, gifted with divine properties, humbles itself. The humiliation of Christ is only an attribute of the incarnate one, not, however, of the Logos itself per se. Humiliation means not exercising the divine properties through the human nature during the period of the earthly life of Jesus. Here there is a question about how to understand this "not exercising." Does it mean a real renunciation, an emptying of the divine properties through the humiliation, or does it mean a concealing, not allowing the divine powers in Jesus to become visible? So the doctrine of the two states leads to the controversy of the kenoticists and crypticists. Those who hold the former position are called the kenoticists. They emphasize the real renunciation, while the crypticists refer to a concealing. The crypticists press for the identity of the incarnate one, as he is in eternity, with the God-human, as he is the humiliated one. The risen one and the humiliated one must be the same, otherwise all is lost. The one who had to suffer is at the same time the one who must not be able to suffer. Against this arises the objection that if this were so, then Christ would not have really suffered, nor would he have really died. According to Philippians 2, it has much more to do with a real *kenosis* or self-emptying. Christ has really died. Christ has confined the use of his divine properties entirely to himself.

The crypticists and kenoticists then agreed to an unimpressive formula: The humiliated Christ has used the divine properties when he wanted and not used them when he wanted. The entire Christological problem is shifted here to another level. It has to do with the one God-human but in two different states and with the identity of the God-human but still in the twofold form of the God-human, concealed and visible.

The doctrine of the kenosis is for the Lutheran dogmatics a necessary completion of the *genus majestaticum,* which the kenoticists put alongside a *genus tapeinoticum,* the category that relates to the humiliation. Thereby at the same time they initiated a rejection of the doctrine of the two natures in general.

The Chalcedonian formula is an answer to the how question. But in this answer, the how question presents itself as overcome. In the Chalcedonian formula the doctrine of the two natures has prevailed. It is valid to develop further this interpretation of the Chalcedonian formula. That can only happen if one has gotten beyond thinking about the divinity and humanity as something ready to hand and if thought does not commence with the isolated natures but with the reality that Jesus Christ *is* God. One may no further interpret that *is.* That has been established by God and therefore is presupposed in all our thinking. It can never be construed after the fact.

After the Chalcedonian formula one may therefore no longer ask how to think about the difference of the natures and the unity of the person, but rather: Who is this human being about whom it is said that he is God?

Dietrich Bonhoeffer, Christology Lectures, 1933
(DBW 12:332–334, 336)

Let the same mind be in you that was in
Christ Jesus,
who, though he was in the form of God,
did not regard equality with God
as something to be exploited,
but emptied himself,
taking the form of a slave,
being born in human likeness.
And being found in human form,
he humbled himself
and became obedient to the point of death—
even death on a cross.

Therefore God also highly exalted him
and gave him the name
that is above every name,
so that at the name of Jesus
every knee should bend,
in heaven and on earth and under the earth,
and every tongue should confess
that Jesus Christ is Lord,
to the glory of God the Father.

Paul's Letter to the Philippians 2:5–11

Who is this God? God is the one who has become human, just as we have become human. He is entirely human. Therefore nothing human is foreign to him. Just as I am a human being, so has Jesus Christ also become a human being. We say about this human being, Jesus Christ, that he is God. Thereby we do not mean that we already knew beforehand who God might be. Nor do we mean that the statement that this human being is God attaches something additional to his being as a human. God and human are not to be combined into a natural concept. The statement that this human being is God is intended to mean something entirely different. The divine being of this human being is not something additional to the human being of Jesus Christ. This statement, that this human being is God, occurs vertically from above, a statement that pertains to Jesus Christ, the human being. It neither adds nor detracts something from Jesus Christ, but qualifies the entire human being as God. It is God's judgment about this human being! It is God's Word that qualifies this human being, Jesus Christ, as God. But the essential difference from all other human beings is that the Word of God descending here from above in Jesus Christ is Godself. Therefore, because Jesus is God's judgment about Godself, he points at the same time to himself and to God.

Thereby the attempt at trying to unify two isolated and perceptible realities is finally set aside. Jesus the human being is believed in as God, precisely as *the* human being, not in spite of his humanity or by overlooking his humanity. Faith is ignited in Jesus Christ, the human being. Jesus Christ is God not in his divine nature, but is God only in faith, thus no longer in a localized and describable way. If Jesus Christ should be described as God, one may not speak of his omnipotence or omniscience, but rather of his manger and his cross.

The child in the manger is God. If someone should speak about the human being, Jesus Christ, as about God, one may not talk about him as a representative of a God concept, i.e., in his omniscience or omnipotence but about his weakness and manger.

The incarnate God is the glorified one. God is glorified in the human being. That is the final mystery of the Trinity. "From now until eternity" God views Godself as the incarnate one. The glorification of God in this human being is at the same time the glorification of humanity itself, who shall have life in eternity with the trinitarian God. It is therefore not right to view the incarnation of God as judgment of human beings. God truly remains still a human being after the judgment. The incarnation of God is the message of God about the glorification of God, who sees honor in being in the form of a human being.

Why does this sound so improbable and strange to us? Because the incarnation of God in Jesus Christ is not the visible glorification of God, for the incarnate one is the crucified one.

Dietrich Bonhoeffer, Christology Lectures, 1933
(DBW 12:340–342)

God's Son became human,
in order that humans
would have a home in God.

Hildegard of Bingen

We conceive no other God than the one,
who is there in that man,
the one who came from heaven.
I begin with the manger.

Martin Luther

Lord Jesus Christ,
You were poor and needy,
As captive and abandoned as I.
You know every need of human beings,
You abide by me,
When no human being stands by me,
You forget me not and you seek me out,
You desire that I know You
And draw me to Yourself.
Lord, I hear Your call and follow.
Help me!

Dietrich Bonhoeffer, "Prayers for Prisoners," 1943
(DBW 8:205)

Wherever the talk is about the humiliation, this is no limiting of the divinity. Humiliation does not mean to be *more* human and *less* God. And risen does not mean being *more* God and *less* human. Jesus remains in humiliation and is risen entirely human and entirely God. The statement, that this one is God, must be made about the humiliated one in the same way as it is about the risen one. Jesus in his death makes nothing of the divine properties visible. To the contrary, he is a dying human being who doubts God. And we say about him, that this one is God. God is not concealed in the human being but rather God is revealed as the God-human. However, this God-human is concealed in the way of existence that is the humiliation.

Who is the humiliated God-human? The doctrines of the incarnation and the humiliation must be kept radically separated. The way of existence that is the humiliation is an act of the God-human. It is not separable temporally from the act of incarnation, but the God-human in history is already the humiliated God-human from the manger to the cross.

How does the special way of existence that is the humiliation express itself? In that he has assumed sinful flesh. In his humiliation Christ, the God-human, goes freely into the world of sin and death. He enters so fully that he is concealed in it and is no longer visibly recognizable as the God-human. He goes incognito as the beggar among beggars and as the exile among exiles, but also as the sinless one among sinners, even more as the sinner among sinners.

The doctrine of the sinlessness of Jesus is the central and decisive point. For the question is this: Has Jesus as the humiliated God-human entirely entered into human sin? Has he been a sinful human being like us? If he has not been that, then has he been a human being at all? And if he has been that, how can he, who was in the same need as us, help us out of our need?

It all depends on how one understands what "form of the flesh" means. This is the real image of human "flesh." The essential of our flesh is its fallibility and self-will. Christ has assumed all the liabilities of human beings. To what degree then is he distinct from us? In the first place, not at all.

He is a human being like us and is tempted as we are. But also there was at work in his flesh a law that ran counter to the will of God. He existed continually in a struggle. He even did what looked like sin. He was harsh to his mother in the temple, he evaded his opponents, and he summoned resistance against the ruling caste of the pious and their followers. He must have been a sinner in the eyes of others. He entered to the point of being unrecognizable.

Yet it all comes down to the fact that *he* is the one who enters there and who does this and that, which the spectator of his life can only judge as trespasses. And because *he* is the one, the accusations shine in another light. *He* had fear like us, was tempted exactly like us, and therefore stands under the same condemnation. But because *he* stands under the same condemnation as us, thereby are we saved. As the one *he* is, *he* had fear like us human beings. Due to the one *he* is, we must endure and risk all these most provocative accusations about this humiliated God-human.

He was made sin for us. Luther says that he is himself a robber, murderer, and adulterer like us, because he bears our sin. But at the same time *he* is the sinless one, the holy one, the eternal one, the Lord, the Son of his Father.

There can be no agreement between these two assertions, as if one still could tear the humiliated Jesus out of the "form of the flesh." He is in the form of the flesh although without sin, tempted as we are in the form of the flesh yet without sin. The statement about sinlessness goes awry, if it takes into consideration the tangible deeds of Jesus.

These deeds took place in the form of the flesh. One can and should be able to look at them ambiguously, seeing good and evil. If someone wants to be incognito, then you insult that one if you say, "I have recognized you at once." Therefore we should not base his sinlessness on his deeds. The assertion of the sinlessness of Jesus according to his deeds is not a morally tangible judgment, but is recognized in faith, that *he* is the one who does these deeds, *he* who is eternally without sin. The assertion of the sinlessness of Jesus is no moral assertion, but is recognized in faith.

Dietrich Bonhoeffer, Christology Lectures, 1933
(DBW 12:343–345)

Because Jesus is not about the proclamation and realization of new ethical ideals, nor about his own moral purity, but only about love for real human beings, therefore he is able to enter into communion with their guilt. . . . Out of his selfless love and his sinlessness, Jesus enters into the guilt of humanity, taking it upon himself. . . . Whoever wants to escape from responsibility for guilt withdraws . . . from the redeeming mystery of Jesus Christ's sinless guilt offering and has no share in the divine justification, which is based on this event. Someone like this puts personal innocence over responsibility for humanity and is blind to the enormous guilt that is thereby taken upon oneself.

Dietrich Bonhoeffer, *Ethics,* 1942
(DBW 6:275f.)

You who will emerge from the flood,
In which we have gone under,
Remember
When you speak of our failings
The dark time too
Which you have escaped.
For we went, changing countries oftener
than our shoes
Through the wars of the classes, despairing
When there was injustice only, and no
rebellion.

And yet we know:
Hatred, even of meanness
Contorts the features.
Anger, even against injustice
Makes the voice hoarse. Oh, we
Who wanted to prepare the ground for
friendliness
Could not ourselves be friendly.

But you, when the time comes at last
And man is a helper to man
Think of us
With forbearance.

Bertolt Brecht, To Those Born Later, 1947

The humiliated God-human is the scandal of
the pious and really of human beings in general.
The most inconceivable idea for the pious is the
claim that this human being advanced, that he
was not only a pious one but God's Son. Thereby
he asserted his authority, "But I say to you . . ."
and, "Your sins are forgiven." If Jesus' nature
were divinized, one would need to take this claim

for granted. If he had done signs as they were demanded of him, one would have had to believe him. But exactly at the crucial point, he backs off. And that creates the scandal. But everything depends on this fact. If he had answered the question that was directed at him about his being the Christ by working a miracle, then the assertion would no longer be valid that he has become a human being like us, for then there would be an exception on the decisive point. Therefore the more impenetrable his incognito, the more persistent the question about his being the Christ.

This means that the form of the stumbling block is the only form in which Christ makes faith possible. That means that the form of the scandal of Christ is the form of Christ *pro nobis*. Because Jesus wants to be our freedom, he must become a scandal to us before he becomes salvation for us. Only in the humiliation can he become p*ro nobis*. If Christ had proven himself through a miracle, we would believe, to be sure. But Christ would not then be our salvation, for it would then not be faith in the incarnate God, but the acknowledgment of an apparently supernatural fact. But that is not faith. Faith occurs when I so abandon myself to God that I risk my life at God's Word, exactly at that place where it is contrary to every visible appearance. Only when I renounce visible testimony do I believe in God. The only assurance that faith endures is the Word of God itself.

Christ *pro nobis* is the Christ who reconciles me to God, and that occurs only through this scandal and completely through faith. The scandal that we experience is the continuous temptation of the faith. This, however, teaches us to pay attention to the Word. Faith comes out of temptation.

Dietrich Bonhoeffer, Christology Lectures, 1933
(DBW 12:345f.)

Before God and beside God we live without God. God lets Godself be driven out of the world onto the cross. God is impotent and weak in the world, and exactly in this way alone God is with us and helps us. Matt. 8:17 makes it very clear that Christ does not help by the power of his omnipotence but by the power of his weakness and his suffering! Here is found the decisive difference from all religions. The religiosity of human beings directs them in their need to the power of God in the world. . . . The Bible directs human beings to the impotence and suffering of God; only the suffering God can help. Insofar as one can agree to the development of the world's coming of age, which does away with a false concept of God, the way is made free for the God of the Bible, who attains power and space through his impotence in the world. It is surely here that the "worldly interpretation" will have to begin.

Dietrich Bonhoeffer, "Letter from Tegel Prison," 1944
(DBW 8:534f.)

The humiliated one is *pro nobis* only as the risen one. Only through Christ as the resurrected one and risen one do we know this incognito God-human. We have the one who was born as a child as the eternally present one, the one who bears our guilt as the sinless one. Thus the statement must be reversed: We have the risen one only as the crucified one. We cannot circumvent the scandal by means of the resurrection. Even the resurrected one remains a scandal for us. If he were not that, he would not be for us. The resurrection of Jesus is not the overcoming of his incognito. The resurrection of Jesus will only be believed where the scandal of Jesus Christ is not eliminated. Only the disciples see the Son. It is blind faith that here sees, because they become as those who believe without seeing and thereby those who do see, by faith in his glorification.

Now between humiliation and his being raised there exists the historical fact of the empty tomb. In light of the report of the resurrection, what should we make of the report of the empty tomb? It appears as if our "faith in the resurrection" is tied to the report of the empty tomb. If the tomb were not empty, our faith would not exist.

This is the final scandal that we must endure as those believing in Christ. It remains a scandal on all sides. The impossible possibility that the tomb was empty is a scandal to the faith. Who will then prove that the disciples of Jesus have not discovered his body? Here we cannot get around the scandal. Jesus remains incognito, in the form of the scandal, to the very end, due to the empty tomb. Jesus does not remove his incognito, not even as the resurrected one. He first will lay it aside, when he comes again at the last judgment. Here he will come visibly as the eternal one, the incarnate one, in divine power and glory.

His church goes with the humiliated Christ into humiliation. It can attain no visible verification of its essence, for he has relinquished such. It may also not, as a humiliated church, look upon itself in vain self-satisfaction, as if humiliation were the visible proof that Christ were with it. Here there is no law, and Christ's humiliation is no principle that the church would have to follow, but rather a fact. For the church can be exalted or it can be lowly, if either of these occurs for the sake of Christ. It is not good for the church to praise itself prematurely for its lowliness. Nor is it good for the church to praise itself prematurely for its greatness and power, because it is only good for the church to allow the forgiveness of its sins.

As the presence of the incarnate, humiliated, resurrected, and raised Jesus Christ, the church must also receive from Christ each day anew the will of God. Christ will also each day anew become an offense to its own wishes and hopes. The church must each day anew take exception to the saying: "You will all take offense at me." And it must hold close to the promise: "Blessed is the one who takes no offense at me."

Dietrich Bonhoeffer, Christology Lectures, 1933
(DBW 12:347f.)

The church's commission, upon which its freedom is founded, consists in delivering the message of the free grace of God to all people in Christ's stead and therefore in the ministry of his own Word and work through sermon and sacrament.

We reject the false doctrine, as though the church in human arrogance could place the Word and work of the Lord in the service of any arbitrarily chosen desires, purposes, and plans.

Thesis 6 of the "Barmen Theological Declaration,"
1934

There remains an experience of incomparable worth: that we have learned to see the great events of world history uniquely from the underside, from the perspective of the excluded ones, the suspects, the abused, the powerless, and the derided, in short, from the point of view of the suffering ones. If only during this time neither bitterness nor envy had devoured the heart! If only we view great and small, happiness and unhappiness, strength and weakness, with new eyes! If only our perspective on greatness, humaneness, law, and mercy has become clearer, freer, and less corruptible! If only we see that personal suffering is a more fitting key and fruitful principle for an attentive and engaged interpretation of the world than personal happiness! It all depends on this perspective from the underside not becoming an excuse to be always discontented. Rather we, due to a deeper contentment that is genuinely rooted beyond underside and privilege, must be able to be reconciled to life in all of its dimensions, and to affirm it as such.

Dietrich Bonhoeffer, "Letters and Papers from Prison"
(DBW 8:38f.)

All that we rightly expect from God, all that we may ask of God, is to be found in Jesus Christ. All that a God can and must be able to do, at least as we imagine it, has nothing to do with the God of Jesus Christ. We must immerse ourselves ever again very deeply and very calmly in the life, speaking, acting, suffering, and dying of Jesus, in order to recognize what God promises and fulfills. It is certain that we can always live in the nearness and the presence of God and that this life is for us an entirely new life. There is nothing impossible for us, because for God nothing is impossible. There is no earthly power that can touch us apart from God's will. Danger and need only drive us closer to God. It is certain that we have no claim on anything, yet may ask everything of God. It is certain that our joy is hidden in suffering and our life in dying. It is certain that in all things we are standing in a company that bears us along. To all of this God has spoken in Jesus a *yes* and *amen*. This *yes* and *amen* are the firm ground upon which we stand.

Again and again in these turbulent times we lose sight of why it is really worthwhile to be alive. We think that because this or that person is alive, it also makes sense for us to be alive. In truth, however, it is rather the case that because the earth was deemed worthy to bear the human being, Jesus Christ, because a human being like Jesus has lived, then and only then does it make sense for us human beings to live. If Jesus had not lived, then in spite of all the other human beings whom we know, honor, and love, our life would be senseless.

Dietrich Bonhoeffer, "Letters and Papers from Prison"
(DBW 8:572f.)

The church is only the church when it is there for others. . . . It must participate in the worldly affairs of the human social order, not ruling but helping and serving. It must say to human beings

of all occupations what a life with Christ is, what
it means "to be there for others."

Dietrich Bonhoeffer, "Outline of a Project," 1944
(DBW 8:560)

By Gracious Powers: A Poem

By gracious powers so wonderfully sheltered,
And confidently waiting come what may,
We know that God is with us night and morning,
And never fails to greet us each new day.

Yet is this heart by its old foe tormented,
Still evil days bring burdens hard to bear;
Oh, give our frightened souls the sure salvation,
For which, O Lord, you taught us to prepare.

And when this cup you give is filled to brimming
With bitter suffering, hard to understand,
We take it thankfully and without trembling
Out of so good and so beloved a hand.

Yet when again in this same world you give us
The joy we had, the brightness of your sun,
We shall remember all the days we lived through
And our whole life shall then be yours alone.

By gracious powers so faithfully protected,
So quietly, so wonderfully near,
I'll live each day in hope, with you beside me,
And go with you through every coming year.

Dietrich Bonhoeffer, "Letters and Papers from Prison"
(DBW 8:607f)

Acknowledgments

Bonhoeffer citations are taken from Dietrich Bonhoeffer Werke (DBW), 16 volumes, Munich/Gütersloh: Chr. Kaiser Verlag, 1986-1998: DBW 6: *Ethik;* DBW 8: *Widerstand und Ergebung: Briefe und Aufzeichnungen aus der Haft;* DBW 12: *Berlin 1932-1933;* DBW 14: *Illegale Theologenausbildung: Finkenwalde 1935-1937;* DBW 15: *Illegale Theologenausbildung: Sammelvikariate 1937-1940.* Except where noted below, all translations from the German are by Craig L. Nessan, including that of the essay by Renate Wind.

"Barmen Theological Declaration," taken from Arthur C. Cochrane, *The Church's Confession under Hitler.* Philadelphia: Westminster, 1962.

Saint Joan of the Stockyards, in Bertold Brecht, *Seven Plays.* Edited and with an introduction by Eric Bentley. New York: Grove Press, 1961.

"To Those Born Later," in Bertolt Brecht, *Poems 1913-1956.* Edited by John Willett and Ralph Manheim. New York: Methuen, 1976.

"By Gracious Powers," in *With One Voice: A Lutheran Resource for Worship.* Hymn text 736 translated by Fred Pratt Green. Minneapolis: Augsburg Fortress, 1995.

Notes

1. Letter to Karl-Friedrich Bonhoeffer, quoted by Eberhard Bethge, *Dietrich Bonhoeffer: A Biography,* rev. and ed. Victoria J. Barnett (Minneapolis: Fortress, 2000), 205f.

2. E. Bethge, R. Bethge, and Chr. Gremmels, eds., *Dietrich Bonhoeffer: A Life in Pictures,* trans. John Bowden (Philadelphia: Fortress, 1986), 74.

3. Dietrich Bonhoeffer, "Die Kirche vor der Judenfrage," in C. Nicolaisen and E.A. Scharffenorth, eds., *Berlin 1932–1933, Dietrich Bonhoeffer Werke* (Gütersloh: Chr. Kaiser, 1989), 12:353f.

4. "Letter to Reinhold Niebuhr, February 6, 1933," in ibid, 12:51.

5. Otto Dudzus, "Nachwort," in Dietrich Bonhoeffer, *Christologie* (Munich: Chr. Kaiser, 1972), 94.

6. Bethge, *Dietrich Bonhoeffer,* 322.

7. Bonhoeffer, *Berlin,* 204f.

8. Ibid, 210.

9. Bethge, *Dietrich Bonhoeffer,* 228.

10. Tiemo Rainer Peters in *Dietrich Bonhoeffer: Gefahrdetes Erbe in bedrohter Welt* (Berlin/GDR: Union-Verlag, 1987), 71.

11. Bethge, *Dietrich Bonhoeffer,* 650.

12. Albrecht Schoenherr, "Dietrich Bonhoeffer und der Weg der Kirche in der DDR," in *Bonhoeffer-Studien* (Berlin: Union-Verlag, 1985), 153.

13. Georges Casalis, "Dietrich et Camilo," *Christianisme au XX. siecle,* April 7, 1986.

14. Tiemo Rainer Peters, *Die Dimension des Politischen in der Theologie Dietrich Bonhoeffers* (Munich/Mainz: Grünewald Verlag, 1976), 50.

15. Ibid., 202.

16. William Hamilton, "A Secular Theology for a World Come of Age," *Theology Today* 18(Jan 62):435-459.

17. Ibid., 445.

18. Ibid, 458f.

19. John A. T. Robinson, *Honest to God* (Philadelphia: Westminster, 1963).

20. Ibid, 77.

21. David L. Edwards, ed., *The Honest to God Debate: Some Reactions to the Book "Honest to God"* (Philadelphia: Westminster, 1963).

22. Paul M. van Buren, *The Secular Meaning of the Gospel: Based on an Analysis of Its Language* (New York: Macmillan, 1963), 18.

23. Harvey Cox, *The Secular City: Secularization and Urbanization in Theological Perspective* (New York: Macmillan, 1965), 2, 211–13.

24. Thomas J. J. Altizer, "Word and History," in Thomas J. J. Altizer and William Hamilton, *Radical Theology and the Death of God* (Indianapolis: Bobbs-Merril, 1966), 135–36. See also William Hamilton's essay in the same volume, "Dietrich Bonhoeffer," 113–18.

25. Eberhard Bethge, *Bonhoeffer: Exile and*

Martyr (London: Collins, 1975), 24.

26. Edwin H. Robertson, "Bonhoeffer's Christology," introduction to Dietrich Bonhoeffer, *Christ the Center,* trans. John Bowden (New York: Harper & Row, 1966), 9.

27. John Godsey, Review of *Christ the Center, Journal of Religion* 47 (April 67): 152.

28. William J. Hill, Review of *Christ the Center, Theological Studies* 27 (1966): 691.

29. Thomas E. Ambrogi, Review of *Christ the Center, Una Sancta* 24 (1967): 78.

30. Clifford Green, "Sociality and Church in Bonhoeffer's 1933 Christology," *Scottish Journal of Theology* 21 (1968): 416–34.

31. Dietrich Bonhoeffer, *Christ the Center,* trans. Edwin H. Robertson (San Francisco: Harper & Row, 1978).

32. William Blair Gould, *The Worldly Christian: Bonhoeffer on Discipleship* (Philadelphia: Fortress, 1967); and Geffrey B. Kelly, *Liberating Faith: Bonhoeffer's Message for Today* (Minneapolis: Augsburg, 1984).

33. John De Gruchy, ed., *Dietrich Bonhoeffer: Witness to Jesus Christ* (London: Collins, 1988; Minneapolis: Fortress, 1991); and Geffrey B. Kelly and F. Burton Nelson, eds., *A Testament to Freedom: The Essential Writings of Dietrich Bonhoeffer* (San Francisco: HarperSanFrancisco, 1990).

34. Bonhoeffer, *Christ the Center,* 78.

35. Robert McAfee Brown, ed., *Kairos: Three Prophetic Challenges* (Grand Rapids: Eerdmans, 1990).

36. *On the Way: From Kairos to Jubilee* (Chicago: Kairos/USA, 1994).

Further Reading

Bethge, Eberhard. *Dietrich Bonhoeffer: A Biography*. Revised and edited by Victoria J. Barnett. Minneapolis: Fortress Press, 2000.

Bonhoeffer, Dietrich. *A Testament to Freedom: The Essential Writings of Dietrich Bonhoeffer*. Edited by Geffrey B. Kelly and F. Burton Nelson. San Francisco: HarperSanFrancisco, 1990.

Bonhoeffer, Dietrich. *Letters and Papers from Prison*. Translated by Reginald Fuller and John Bowden. New York: Collier Books, 1971.

Bonhoeffer, Dietrich. *Temptation & Creation and Fall: Two Biblical Studies*. Translated by John C. Fletcher and Kathleen Downham. New York: Touchstone Books, 1959.

Bonhoeffer, Dietrich. *Dietrich Bonhoeffer Works,* Volume 4: *Discipleship*. Translated by Barbera Green and Reinhard Krauss. Minneapolis: Fortress Press, 2001.

Bonhoeffer, Dietrich. *Dietrich Bonhoeffer Works,* Volume 5: *Life Together, Prayerbook of the Bible*. Translated by Daniel W. Bloesch and James

H. Burtness. Minneapolis: Fortress Press, 1996.

Bonhoeffer, Dietrich. *The Wisdom and Witness of Dietrich Bonhoeffer*. Meditations by Wayne Whitson Floyd. Minneapolis: Fortress Press, 2000.

De Gruchy, John W., ed. *Bonhoeffer for a New Day: Theology in a Time of Transition*. Grand Rapids: Eerdmans Publishing Co., 1997.

Feil, Ernst. *The Theology of Dietrich Bonhoeffer*. Translated by Martin Rumscheidt. Philadelphia: Fortress Press, 1985.

Green, Clifford J. *Bonhoeffer: A Theology of Sociality*. Grand Rapids: Eerdmans Publishing Co., 1999.

Marsh, Charles. *Reclaiming Dietrich Bonhoeffer: The Promise of His Theology*. New York: Oxford University Press, 1994.

Rasmussen, Larry, with Renate Bethge. *Dietrich Bonhoeffer – His Significance for North Americans*. Minneapolis: Fortress Press, 1991.

Wind, Renate. *Dietrich Bonhoeffer: A Spoke in the Wheel*. Translated by John Bowden. Grand Rapids: Eerdmans Publishing Co., 1991.

Craig L. Nessan is Academic Dean and Associate Professor of Contextual Theology at Wartburg Theological Seminary and the author of *Beyond Maintenance to Mission: A Theology of the Congregation* (Fortress Press, 1999).

Renate Wind is Professor of Religious Education at the Fachhochschule Nuremberg in Germany.